SMART WORDS READERS

FISH

Christine A. Caputo

SCHOLASTIC INC.

What are SMART WORDS?

Smart Words are frequently used words that are critical to understanding concepts taught in the classroom. The more Smart Words a child knows, the more easily he or she will grasp important curriculum concepts. Smart Words Readers introduce these key words in a fun and motivational format while developing important literacy skills. Each new word is highlighted, defined in context, and reviewed. Engaging activities at the end of each chapter allow readers to practice the words they have learned.

ISBN 978-0-545-46700-1

Packaged by Q2A Bill Smith

Copyright © 2012 by Scholastic Inc.

Picture Credit: t= top, b= bottom, l= left, r= right, c= center

Cover Page: Luis Fernando Curci Chavier/Shutterstock.
Title Page: Rich Carey/Shutterstock.
Content Page: Stormcab/Shutterstock.

4: Rich Carey/Shutterstock; 5: 4FR-Photography (Nils Kahle)/Istockphoto; 6: Rob & Ann Simpson/Visuals Unlimited/Corbis; 7: Natalia Macheda/Shutterstock; 8: Nataliia Melnychuk/Shutterstock; 9: DmZ/Shutterstock; 10: Brandon D. Cole/Encyclopedia/Corbis; 11: Tenn Hian-kun; 12: Kutlayev Dmitry/Shutterstock; 13: Eric Isselee/Fotolia; 14c: Krzysztof Odziomek/Istockphoto; 14b: Faup/Shutterstock; 15: Daniel Zuckerkandel/Shutterstock; 16: Vilainecrevette/Shutterstock; 17: Willyam Bradberry/Shutterstock; 19t: Manda Nicholls/Shutterstock; 19c: Wim van Egmond/Visuals Unlimited/Corbis; 19b: Peter Reynolds/Frank Lane Picture Agency/Documentary Value/Corbis; 20: Specta/Shutterstock; 21: Shane Gross/Shutterstock; 24: Cathysbelleimage/Dreamstime; 26: Peter Essick/Aurora Photos/Corbis; 27: Patrick Endres/Visuals Unlimited/Corbis; 28: AJP/Shutterstock; 29: Richard Herrmann/Visuals Unlimited/Corbis.

Q2A Bill Smith Art Bank: 5, 7, 18-19, 22-23, 25.

12 11 10 9 8 7   14 15 16 17/0

Printed in the U.S.A.   40
First printing, September 2012

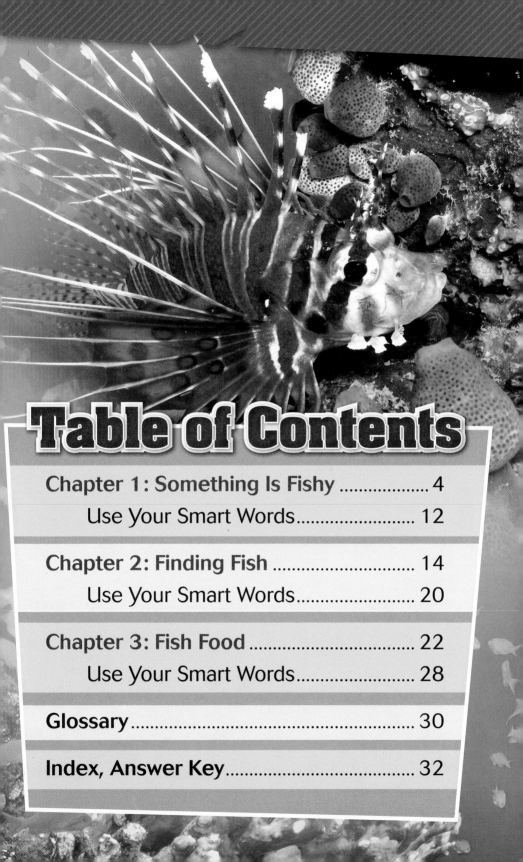

Table of Contents

Chapter 1: Something Is Fishy 4

    Use Your Smart Words........................ 12

Chapter 2: Finding Fish 14

    Use Your Smart Words........................ 20

Chapter 3: Fish Food 22

    Use Your Smart Words........................ 28

Glossary 30

Index, Answer Key.............................. 32

Something Is Fishy

A colorful angelfish. A tiny minnow. A huge whale shark. What do these animals have in common? They are all **fish**! What makes a fish a fish? Fish have traits, or characteristics, that make them different from all other kinds of animals. Let's find out more about these traits!

Anthias, pufferfish, and cardinalfish all share traits that make them fish.

How to Spot a Fish

Look for these traits:
- lives in water
- has gills
- is an ectotherm
- has a backbone
- has fins

Fish Alert!
Can all animals that live in water be called fish? No! Whales, dolphins, seals, and sea lions all live in water. But they are not fish. A fish will have all of the traits you see in the box to the left. Other animals that live in water may have some, but not all, of these traits.

All fish live in water. Fish cannot take oxygen from the air like animals that live on land can. To be able to breathe under water, fish have structures called gills.

To see a fish's gills, you need to look on the sides of a fish's body near the back of its head. They look a little like filters. When water flows across the gills, oxygen passes from the water into the fish.

gills

Fish take in water by mouth. The water flows over the gills.

SMART WORDS

fish an ectothermic vertebrate with gills and fins that lives in water

gills body structures that act like filters to move oxygen from the water into the body of an animal living in the water

Keep Your Cool

Whether it's cold or hot outside, your body temperature stays about the same — 98.6°F (37°C). That's because people are **endotherms**. Endotherms maintain a constant body temperature.

Fish are **ectotherms**. The body temperature of a fish depends on its surroundings. If the water is warm, the fish is warm. If the water is cold, the fish is cold.

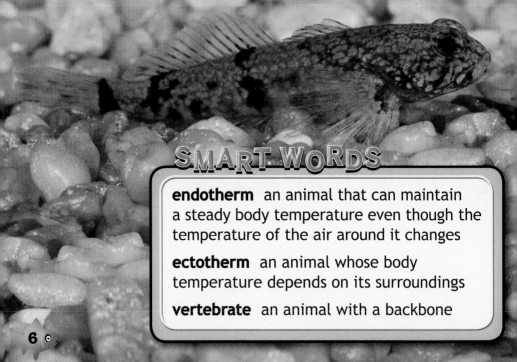

This sculpin swims to the cold bottom of a lake to cool off. It swims back up to the warm water near the surface to warm up.

SMART WORDS

endotherm an animal that can maintain a steady body temperature even though the temperature of the air around it changes

ectotherm an animal whose body temperature depends on its surroundings

vertebrate an animal with a backbone

All Those Bones

No matter how different some might look, all fish are **vertebrates**. A vertebrate is an animal that has a backbone. A backbone is made up of individual bones. These bones are a framework that protect the soft insides of the fish. But they can also bend as the fish moves. This helps the fish to swim.

backbone

The ocean sunfish can grow to more than 10 feet (3 meters) long and can weigh more than 4,900 pounds (2,223 kilograms). It's the largest bony fish in the ocean!

Scales and Fins

When you think about fish, you might picture layers of shiny scales on their bodies. Scales are a trait that most, but not all, fish have. Scales are thin, flat, overlapping pieces of hard skin that cover a fish's body. They help to protect the fish from harm.

Unlike the scales of lizards and other reptiles, fish scales feel slimy. Fish produce a substance that forms a thick layer when it touches water. This slimy layer helps protect the fish from infection. It also helps the fish take in oxygen and glide through the water.

Scales can be shaped like diamonds or cones, or they can be round.

Fish use **fins** to move, stay balanced, and even build nests. Fins are fan-shaped structures. They can be on the top, bottom, back, or sides of the fish. Different kinds of fins work together as a fish moves. Some fins appear alone, but others come in pairs.

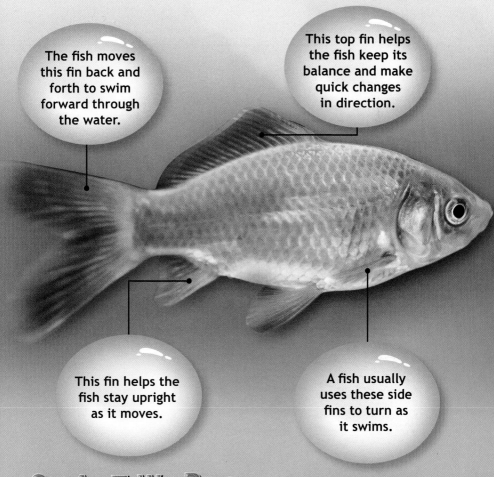

The fish moves this fin back and forth to swim forward through the water.

This top fin helps the fish keep its balance and make quick changes in direction.

This fin helps the fish stay upright as it moves.

A fish usually uses these side fins to turn as it swims.

SMART WORDS

scales thin, flat, overlapping pieces of hard skin that cover the bodies of most fish

fin a structure on a fish that can help it move, steer, or stay balanced

Fish Families

What do fish have in common with birds? They both **hatch** from eggs! Unlike eggs on land, fish eggs do not have a shell. The jelly-like egg contains the baby fish along with the food it needs to develop. When it is ready, the young fish hatches out of the egg.

Ponds, lakes, and oceans can be dangerous places for eggs. Eggs are delicious treats for other animals, including other fish!

A single fish may lay hundreds or even thousands of eggs at one time.

eggs

The paradise fish builds a nest out of bubbles among the floating plants near the surface of the water.

Fish take care of their eggs in different ways. Some fish stand guard around their eggs to make sure other animals don't eat them.

A few kinds of fish build nests out of bubbles. Some fish build nests of sand and gravel. Others build nests with plant materials and mud. Some fish don't build nests at all, so they carry the eggs in their mouths until they hatch.

SMART WORD

hatch to break out of an egg

Use your SMART WORDS

Answer each question with the correct Smart Word.

| fish | gills | endotherm | ectotherm |
| vertebrate | scales | fin | hatch |

1. What are thin, flat, overlapping pieces of hard skin that cover a fish's body?

2. What term describes an animal whose temperature changes with its surroundings?

3. What term describes an animal that can maintain a steady body temperature?

4. What is an animal that has a backbone, breathes in water, and has fins?

5. What do young fish do when they break out of their egg?

6. What term describes any animal that has a backbone?

7. Through which structures does a fish take oxygen from water?

8. What is a structure on a fish that helps it move and keep its balance?

Answers on page 32

Talk Like a Scientist

You are taking a boat ride on a lake. Your friend asks you to point out the fish. Use your Smart Words to explain how you identify fish in nature.

SMART FACTS

Did You Know?

The marbled hatchetfish is found in rivers throughout South America. They tend to live in large groups.

That's Amazing!

Some fish can jump out of the water, but the marbled hatchetfish is the only fish that can actually fly for short distances by flapping two of its fins like wings!

Good to Know

The marbled hatchetfish is usually only about 1.4 inches (3.5 centimeters) long.

Chapter 2

Finding Fish

Fish need to live in a water habitat. Many fish live in saltwater habitats, or water that contains a significant amount of salt. Oceans are saltwater habitats. Cod, tuna, yellowtail, and halibut are examples of saltwater fish.

Freshwater is water that has very little, if any, salt in it. Rivers, streams, ponds, and marshes are usually freshwater habitats. Catfish, pike, shad, and bass are examples of freshwater fish.

Pike live in freshwater rivers and lakes in North America, Asia, and Europe.

The ghost pipefish lives in the salty Pacific Ocean near Asia.

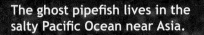

There are a few fish that can survive in both types of water. For example, salmon live in salt water most of the time, but they swim into freshwater to lay eggs. The freshwater is gentler on the delicate eggs.

Other kinds of fish live in estuaries for much of their lives. An **estuary** is a place where the freshwater of a river or stream empties into the salt water of an ocean. Estuaries are sometimes known as "nurseries of the sea" because they provide safe places for fish to build nests and find food.

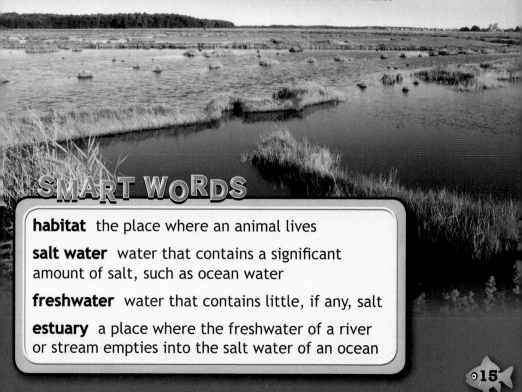

Estuaries often have trees and other plants whose roots give young fish places to hide from birds and other animals.

SMART WORDS

habitat the place where an animal lives

salt water water that contains a significant amount of salt, such as ocean water

freshwater water that contains little, if any, salt

estuary a place where the freshwater of a river or stream empties into the salt water of an ocean

Inside a Coral Reef

A **coral reef** is a saltwater habitat formed by tiny aquatic animals called coral polyps. A coral polyp looks like a small, round circle. When a coral polyp dies, it leaves its skeleton behind. Young coral polyps attach to the skeletons and form their own skeletons.

Slowly, over hundreds or thousands of years, the skeletons build up to form an amazing structure known as a coral reef. The reef grows upward toward the surface of the water. There may be millions of coral polyps in a single coral reef.

Coral reefs are found in the warm areas of the southern Pacific Ocean, Red Sea, Caribbean Sea, and the Indian Ocean.

Yellow clownfish swim among the sea anemone in this coral reef.

The reef provides many great hiding spots for small fish. It also lets fish find food easily. There may be more different kinds of fish, or **diversity**, in a coral reef than in any other fish habitat.

The fish in a coral reef are usually brightly colored. Think of an underwater rainbow! Blue parrot fish, black-and-white clown triggerfish, and blue-gold queen angelfish all live there. So do hammerhead sharks! They are one of the largest fish in a coral reef.

SMART WORDS

coral reef a saltwater habitat that forms in warm ocean waters from the skeletons of small aquatic animals

diversity variety or differences among animals

Zone In

Different kinds of habitats are located throughout Earth's oceans. One major factor that makes ocean habitats different from one another is the amount of sunlight they receive. The ocean can be divided into three layers called **light zones**.

Sunlit Zone — 50–660 feet
- smallest zone
- most sunlight
- 90% of ocean life
- many plants

Twilight Zone — 660–3,300 feet
- darker and colder than sunlit zone
- small amount of light
- fewer fish than sunlit zone
- few plants grow here

Midnight Zone — 3,300–13,000 feet
- deepest and largest zone
- no sunlight – dark!
- extremely cold

stingray

Many fish live in the food-rich sunlit zone. Stingrays, sharks, tuna, and mackerel are just a few.

viper fish

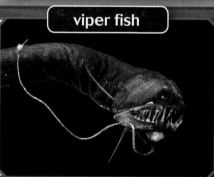

Fish in the twilight zone have a harder time finding food. Some have sharp fangs that help them catch food. They often have large eyes to see in the darkness. Some of the fish in this layer can make their own light to help them find food.

angler fish

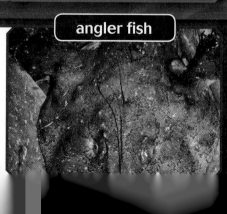

Few fish can survive in this layer. The angler fish has a structure that hangs above its mouth like a fishing lure. When other animals come to the lure, the angler fish swallows them up.

Match each description with the correct Smart Word.

| habitat | salt water | freshwater | estuary |
| coral reef | diversity | light zones |

1. the type of water that makes up Earth's oceans
2. a region where rivers or streams empty into an ocean
3. an underwater habitat made from the skeletons of sea creatures
4. the place where an animal lives
5. variety or differences among animals
6. the layers of sunlight in the ocean
7. the type of water that makes up most rivers, lakes, and streams

Answers on page 32

Talk Like a Scientist

A nature photographer wants to take a trip to see different kinds of fish. Where should the photographer go? Send him an e-mail describing places where fish live. Use your Smart Words.

SMART FACTS

Did You Know?

The whale shark is the largest fish alive. Whale sharks can be up to 40 feet (12.2 meters) long. They can live for over 100 years.

Shark Spotting

Whale sharks live in warm ocean waters. They can often be spotted off the coasts of Australia. These sharks tend to stay near the water's surface.

All Those Teeth!

A whale shark has about 3,000 small teeth set in 300 rows. But it doesn't use the teeth to feed. Instead, it opens its mouths to suck in small animals and fish. Rows of bristles inside the mouth trap the fish, and the water goes out through the gills.

Fish Food

Like all other animals, fish need food to stay alive. No matter what habitat they live in, fish cannot make their own food, so they eat other living things. A **food chain** describes the flow of food from one living thing to another.

In most habitats on Earth, only plants can make food. Tiny plants make food in many aquatic habitats. Tiny animals eat the plants. Small fish then eat the tiny animals. Large fish eat the small fish, larger fish eat those fish, and then the largest fish eat them. When fish die, they decay and become food for the plants.

Fish can be part of many food chains at the same time. A group of food chains that overlap makes up a **food web**.

Here's how a mackerel can belong to a food web. The mackerel eats an anchovy, but it might also eat a herring or a sand lance. A tuna eats the mackerel, but a shark, ray, or billfish might also eat it.

tiny plants

tiny animals

small fish – anchovy

largest fish – shark

larger fish – tuna

large fish – mackerel

SMART WORDS

food chain the flow of food from one living thing to another

food web a group of overlapping food chains in a habitat

Pollution in the Food Web

Dropping trash in an ocean. Dumping chemicals in a river. Spilling oil in an estuary. All of these actions add **pollution** to aquatic habitats. Pollution is any harmful material that can damage a habitat or the things that live there.

Pollution can harm fish in many ways. For example, chemicals added to water can make fish sick or kill them. Chemicals might also kill the plants or other food fish eat. Some kinds of pollution, such as oil, can stop fish from moving normally, finding food, or laying eggs.

Pollution can cause harmful substances to enter into food chains. The substances move from one fish to the next as they eat.

SMART WORD

pollution any harmful material that can damage a habitat or the things that live there

Mercury is a metal that is found in small amounts in soil and rocks. It can also be released into the air when fuels, like coal, are burned in factories. If the mercury gets released into water, it can be taken in by small organisms. When larger fish eat those organisms, they also take in mercury. Now mercury is in the food chain.

People can take in mercury by eating some kinds of fish. Luckily, the government puts out information about the amount of mercury in fish. People can avoid eating fish that have a lot of mercury.

The black dots represent the mercury that is found in the water and in the fish.

Let's Go Fishing!

Grab a fishing pole and some bait, head out to a nearby waterway, and you might catch your dinner! For centuries, people all over the globe have depended on fish as a source of food.

If people have been fishing for all these years, why are there still so many fish? Usually, young fish are born and grow up to replace fish that are caught. When the number of fish that are caught is about the same as the number that are born, the fish **population** stays the same.

These fishermen near Greenland haul in a net full of cod.

In recent years, **overfishing** has upset this natural process. Overfishing happens when people take fish out of a habitat faster than new fish are being born. Overfishing can cause fish to disappear. If the fish are gone, the animals that feed on fish have nothing to eat. They might disappear as well.

How do we get enough fish for people to eat without overfishing? Governments and other groups are working to find answers to this problem.

SMART WORD

population all of the same type of animal living in the same place at the same time

overfishing the act of removing fish from a habitat faster than they can reproduce

Some places have limits on the number of fish that can be caught. In other places, fishing is stopped for some time to allow fish populations to increase.

Use your SMART WORDS

Read each clue. Choose the Smart Word it describes.

food chain   food web   pollution

population   overfishing

1. I am any harmful material that can damage a habitat.

2. I am the number of a kind of fish living in a habitat at the same time.

3. I am the flow of food from one living thing to another.

4. I am what people are doing when they remove too many fish from a habitat.

5. I am all of the overlapping food chains in a habitat.

Answers on page 32

Talk Like a Scientist

Write a letter to a newspaper explaining why you think it is important to protect the habitats where fish live. Use your Smart Words in your letter.

SMART FACTS

Did You Know?

The Atlantic bluefin tuna is one of the largest and fastest fish in the ocean. They average about 6.5 feet (2 meters) long and weigh about 550 pounds (250 kilograms).

An Expensive Fish

Bluefin tuna are fished for their tasty meat. They are used to make some kinds of sushi. One fish can sell for hundreds of thousands of dollars.

A Fish in Trouble

Due to overfishing, populations of Atlantic bluefin tuna have dropped. If strict laws are not enforced to protect them, soon there may be no bluefin tuna left on Earth.

Glossary

coral reef a saltwater habitat that forms in warm ocean waters from the skeletons of small aquatic animals

diversity variety or differences among animals

ectotherm an animal whose body temperature depends on its surroundings

endotherm an animal that can maintain a steady body temperature even though the temperature of the air around it changes

estuary a place where the freshwater of a river or stream empties into the salt water of an ocean

fin a structure on a fish that can help it move, steer, or stay balanced

fish an ectothermic vertebrate with gills and fins that lives in water

food chain the flow of food from one living thing to another

food web a group of overlapping food chains in a habitat

freshwater water that contains little, if any, salt

gills body structures that act like filters to move oxygen from the water into the body of an animal living in the water

habitat the place where an animal lives

hatch to break out of an egg

light zones the layers of sunlight in the ocean

overfishing the act of removing fish from a habitat faster than they can reproduce

pollution any harmful material that can damage a habitat or the things that live there

population all of the same type of animal living in the same place at the same time

salt water water that contains a significant amount of salt, such as ocean water

scales thin, flat, overlapping pieces of hard skin that cover the bodies of most fish

vertebrate an animal with a backbone

Index

backbone   4, 6, 7, 12
coral reef   16, 17, 20
diversity   17, 20
ectotherm   4–6, 12
egg   10–12, 15, 24
endotherm   6, 12
estuary   15, 20, 24
fin   4, 5, 8, 9, 12, 13
food chain   22–25, 28
food web   22–24, 28
freshwater   14, 15, 20
gills   4, 5, 12, 21
habitat   14–18, 20, 22–24, 27, 28

hatch   10–12
light zone   18–20
mercury   25
nest   9, 11, 15
overfishing   27–29
oxygen   5, 8, 12
pollution   24, 25, 28
population   26–29
salt water   14–17
scales   8, 9, 12
surface   6, 11, 16, 21
temperature   6, 12
trait   4, 8
vertebrate   5–7, 12

SMART WORDS Answer Key

Page 12
1. scales, 2. ectotherm, 3. endotherm, 4. fish, 5. hatch, 6. vertebrate, 7. gills, 8. fin

Page 20
1. salt water, 2. estuary, 3. coral reef, 4. habitat, 5. diversity, 6. light zones, 7. freshwater

Page 28
1. pollution, 2. population, 3. food chain, 4. overfishing, 5. food web